From

Rejected

To

Restored

How God Turns Pain To Purpose
And Gives Hope To The Broken

Pauline M. Dillon

FROM REJECTED TO RESTORED. Copyright © 2021. **Pauline M. Dillon.** All Rights Reserved.

Printed in the United States of America.

No portion of this book may be reproduced, stored in a retrieval system, or transmitted in any form or by any means, except for brief quotations in printed reviews, without the prior written permission of DayeLight Publishers or **Pauline M. Dillon**.

PUBLISHERS

ISBN: 978-1-953759-44-3 (paperback)

Scripture quotations marked (NIV) are taken from the Holy Bible, New International Version®, NIV®. Copyright © 1973, 1978, 1984 by Biblica, Inc.™ Used by permission of Zondervan. All rights reserved worldwide.

Acknowledgments

Thanks to Jesus Christ, my Lord and Saviour, for giving me the inspiration to write my first book.

Thanks to my two friends who gave wonderful support, encouragement, prayer, and read and re-read the script.

Thanks to the DayeLight Publishers team for your expertise and help with this project.

God bless you, and thank you all.

Dedication

I want to begin by giving praise and thanks to God, who has kept me and seen me through some very rough and painful times. He has been so very faithful.

This book is dedicated to Him, my Lord and Saviour, JESUS CHRIST. I do not know where I would be without Him and if I would still be in my right mind.

Praise God from whom all my blessings flowed and continue to flow.

Psalm 145 is one of my favourite Psalms. Verse 21a echoes my praise: "My mouth will speak in praise of the Lord…forever and ever."

Table of Contents

Acknowledgments 3

Dedication 5

Foreword 9

Introduction..11

Chapter 1: How It All Started 13

Chapter 2: How I Began To Love Myself 21

Chapter 3: I Had No Father But God 29

Chapter 4: Knowing God's Love 35

Chapter 5: Making A Difference 39

Chapter 6: Ordinary Made Extraordinary 43

Chapter 7: God's Purpose For My Life 51

Conclusion 59

About the Author..61

Foreword

I have known the author for many years through our attendance and involvement at Swallowfield Chapel. We met as adolescents and have maintained our relationship since then through the common bond of our faith as believers in Christ.

For years, Pauline has been journaling the events of her life with the desire to one day publish her story. **From Rejected To Restored: How God Turns Pain To Purpose And Give Hope To The Broken** is a scrupulously honest account of some very intimate details of her life, from the emotional and physical suffering at the hands of her mother, the period of living on the streets at a very young age and then eventually in state care, all leading to a captivating story of a life wonderfully transformed by God. This book will generate a myriad of emotions in its readers—from shock and disbelief to shouts of praise and thanksgiving.

Pauline has not allowed the pain and sorrow experienced in her early years to direct and control her future. She has arisen with tenacity, temerity, and perseverance to shine through with strong faith in her heavenly Father and with the caring support of friends and fellow Christians.

Pauline is a precious gem who her heavenly Father has been refining through her many trials to bring her to a place where she can now share her story with the hope that it will inspire, encourage and motivate others.

Sister In Christ

Introduction

I was born in Kingston, Jamaica, on August 7, 1962, to a teenaged mother: fifteen years old. I was her first child, and she went on to have seven other children. I do not know my father, and even though I know my mother, we were not really connected. I have lived most of my life outside of her after I was put in state care at age eight.

My second birth was my spiritual birth when I accepted the Lord Jesus Christ as my personal Saviour. This was on September 15, 1977, at the age of fifteen. I was later baptized in 1979.

Based on my life's journey and experiences, I felt led by the Lord to chronicle my journey in a book. I started writing this book in 2006. However, very little happened except for jottings for fourteen years. Then in 2020, I was made redundant from my full-time job at my church as one of the administrators. This was a very painful time for me. I did a lot of praying, fasting, and seeking the Lord for my next move, and it was then that the Lord reminded me to work on my book, so here we are.

Chapter 1
How It All Started

My life has been eventful and incredibly challenging, yet now I realize that I am very special in God's eyes. I have been special to God all along the journey of my life. When I think of all I have been through, it is a wonder that I am still alive and sane. In retrospect, I see that God always had a plan for my life. Therefore, even when I did not understand what purpose meant, He was working out His purposes in me through every situation, trial, pain, and darkness I have faced.

The challenges started long ago when I was a child because I was born to a teenaged mother. To this day, I have not experienced or felt the love of my birth mother for me, nor do I understand her. The beatings I received at the hand of my mother were a bit much and very brutal. My mother would beat me all the time for no apparent reason that I can remember. I recall that one time she beat me so badly that I was bleeding all over my body, and it was painful. I felt that every time she beat me, if she did not see blood, she would not stop beating me.

Also, I recall another occasion when I was being beaten (maybe this beating was one of the worst inflicted on me) that my mother took away all the clothes I was wearing so she could beat me naked. This beating went on for hours before a neighbor came over and spoke to her, suggesting that she stop. To this day, I can still hear the words my neighbour spoke to my mother in my head: *"Ava, you have been beating this child all day. Are you not tired? Are you going to kill her? This might be the one child that will feed you one day to come. What has she done that you keep beating her so?"* That was when she stopped. It was almost late evening.

My mother never talked much. She was always so angry, sad, stern, and could be mean and unkind. She would also curse, telling me very unpleasant things. One of the things I recall she would often say is, *"You ugly like you no good father and maybe going to be just as worthless like him."* She did not seem to care very much for me. I never heard the words "I love you" or received any form of affirmation from her (as I reflect, she may have been experiencing abuse from her live-in boyfriend also). As a result of this constant abuse from my mother, I started running away from home at an early age as I was very afraid of her.

I ran away from home repeatedly and mostly stayed on the streets of downtown Kingston in the Coronation Market. I would look out for my mother whenever I was on the run so that when she came to find me, I would hide from her. Oftentimes, she was not able to find me as I would see her long before she saw me, and I ran, not wanting her to see or catch me. I knew that if she caught me and took me home, there would be more beatings. So as I hid under a market stall or under some lady's skirt, I would watch her asking persons in the market if they had seen her daughter, and she would describe me to them. In those days, I was very thin and slender in stature. Without finding me, most times, she would leave only to come back again two or three days later. I still wonder about those days; why would she come looking for me if all she wanted to do was beat me.

While I was on the streets, my meals frequently came from searching in the garbage in the market or leftovers from the kindness of those persons I stayed around. However, in most cases, food for me was rotten fruits or stale food, and my bed was the cold ground or a market stall that was left empty at night.

I remember, after being in the market for a while, there was a lady who showed me kindness. She must have been one of my assigned angels sent from God. Miss Mathie would feed and care for me. She would often question me, wanting to find out why I was on the streets so often and where my family was. Yet, the only thing I could tell her was how afraid I was of my mother and going home because my mother was beating me all the time.

After many repeated episodes of being caught and taken back home, my mother was unable to cope with my running away from home any longer, so she decided to put me in the care of the state. I found out much later that she lied in an interview with the caregiver so the government facility would take me in. I became a ward of the state at the tender age of eight years old.

I was initially put in a Place of Safety on Hagley Park Road, where I remained for about four years. At that government home, things were hard and unpleasant.

Other children, who were bigger than me, would tease me relentlessly. The bullying went beyond words. This caused feelings of depression and rejection. They would pick on me, beat me up, and just gave me a hard time. It was so hard coping; I cried a lot and could not sleep at nights. It was from those days that I practiced to keep myself and did not want to talk to anyone.

In that "Place of Safety," I had to learn to defend myself and keep myself safe. I had to fight to defend my personal space, including the bunk bed assigned to me. The bigger girls sometimes forced me to do things that I found very unpleasant. They also forced me to do the duties assigned to them, and that was when a fight would often break out if I refused.

The housemothers had their favourites, which was never me. They looked after and made sure nothing bad or out of the ordinary would happen to them. So, I remained defenseless and now subjected to their abuse. Though I was in state care, I was still being beaten up and bullied; it never stopped.

Then, one day, I was surprisingly chosen to be adopted by a lady starting a home for girls called the Link (an adoption-like facility). Looking back, the environment in this new home was fresh and clean compared to where I was coming from. In this home, the attitude and treatment I received was more decent, and it felt different in a lot of ways. I never really experienced a real family before, so this seemed like it was leaning towards that experience. We were often allowed to go to school and church on the outside. We could also receive more visits from our relatives, and my mother would visit at times. Her visits, however, were never pleasant for me, and I did not look forward to those visits at all. I was still very much afraid of her and did not want to be near her since we never had any bonding that I can remember.

Life at the Link, which was situated on Maxfield Avenue, was very interesting and more organized and enjoyable in many ways. There were twelve of us girls, and we were treated with much love, respect, and care by the owner, Mrs. King, and her husband. Her husband would come to the home at times to visit with us and call us out one by one to have conversations. He did this on a weekly basis, providing that fatherly figure, support, and encouragement I so desperately craved. This gesture was amazing and gave me the feeling that this might just be what a family should be like if I had one (I really did not recognize that I was experiencing being a part of a family). Considering the experiences I had at the Place of Safety, this was truly different, and it was special. I, however, kept my distance and did not express appreciation or showed that I cared for such attention from him. I stayed far from him and his wife, who was the main person who would interact with each of us children in this new home.

In retrospect, now I realize this was a defense mechanism I was using: to stay far from people so I would not get hurt, but it did hurt, in a way, as I just found it so hard to trust anyone. Those people were nice, kind, and loving towards us girls, but I did not know that then. I was just in too much pain, and the pain blinded my eyes and caused the way I acted towards them. They meant me well, based on their actions; this I am realizing now as I reflect on those days.

Chapter 2
How I Began To Love Myself

Mrs. King treated us like her own family; she made us feel special. She taught me many things. She especially helped me to cope with the rejection issues I was having. We were taken to her home outside of the facility on weekends, where we interacted with her children to form bonds, but I did not feel special or connected. I did not feel like I could fit in with anyone, nor did I connect with the other girls. I was just alone and felt lonely all the time. The other girls seemed to get along with each other very well, but for me, this never happened. It was hard for me to connect.

Looking back now, I seemed to have lived in a bubble all the time, keeping myself locked in my own mind, not letting anyone in. However, in retrospect, I see that

God was there with me even though I did not know or understand anything about God.

Our daily routine was pretty simple: we would wake up, do house duties, such as tidying my shared dorm and cleaning the bathroom, going to school, and participating in extra after-school activities. My activity was dancing, which I loved. I also loved to sit by myself and make notes in my little book. I would dream of a nice place where I could feel happy, not knowing or realizing that happiness was before me there at the Link.

Depression was never far from me. I wondered why so many bad things had happened to me and how I felt so unhappy all the time. I did not feel like my life was worth living. I spent most of my time by myself; I did not trust anyone, and life just seemed unfair, and I wished I was never born. My negative thoughts did not help my mood, and because I never opened up to share with others, life was miserable and unhappy.

The world seemed to be big. I felt hopeless and was just aimlessly living. I even felt like killing myself and did attempt to do that on one occasion; however, God, through the help of a friend, discouraged me from taking such an action. It was then I started hearing about God. I was invited to church by my friend on several occasions, but it was not until one night when they had a crusade at that church that I finally gave my heart to the Lord Jesus Christ. The preacher that night spoke about life after death and hell. I thought if there was a life that would give me more joy than what I was experiencing, I wanted it.

I remember the preacher speaking about hell in such a graphic way. I thought to myself, if my life was so miserable, why would I want to go to that place that this preacher was talking about which seemed so horrible. I sat there thinking. I did not respond on that first night, but when I went back to the home, I felt so scared I could not sleep. I stayed awake all night because of fear.

I went back to that crusade meeting the following night. At the end of the sermon, I was the first to go up when the altar call was made. I wanted this Jesus this preacher was talking about, and I did not want to go to that hell place he spoke about. A lady came and spoke to me, and she led me in a prayer. I asked the Lord Jesus into my heart. Immediately I felt so light, and I thought to myself that all my problems would end. This, however, was naïve thinking, I would later find out. That night I felt like I was walking on air because of how light I felt.

Physically, nothing changed. I still had issues and very low self-esteem. But I started reading my Bible and the salvation package I was given by that lady who spoke to me at the altar. I also followed her encouragement to read the book of John. She also told me to pray daily and spend time with God, but I did not really understand that instruction. Fortunately, I was given some clarity from the friend who had invited me to her church, and I continued to read my Bible daily.

By then, other things were was happening in the home that brought on a drastic change. I cannot say I knew all the details then of what it was, but we girls were all split up from the home to other government homes. We were told our happy home was closing down. I was sent to another Place of Safety that reminded me of the first one I went to initially on Hagley Park Road. The home I was sent to was on Lady Musgrave Road. This home had many more girls, and they were a rough bunch. It was hard there. I could still attend the school that I was going to, but there were many more rules and restrictions at this government home.

The house mothers at this home treated us badly. The food was not cooked properly, and if something was cooked that you did not eat or like, you were forced to eat it anyway or do without. I was sometimes punished for stuff that I did not do. The other girls would tell lies on me, especially if they asked me to do their duties and it was not done before the house mother checked. One of the few positives in this home was that the lady who ran this government home was nice, and we could talk to her about almost anything.

Lots of outside groups came to this home to talk to us children. I still struggled with trusting anyone, so even though I attended the group meetings, I just listened most of the time and did not talk much. However, there was one church group that came a lot, and eventually, I found myself, along with some of the other girls, going to their church. I had told the leader of that group that I wanted to be baptized as she helped me to understand the things of the Lord more.

It was at this church that I was "sort-of" mentored and was taught more about God and how to study the Word of God. I was able to attend Sunday School classes and, WOW, it was an eye-opener! I was about fourteen by now, so I had lots of Sunday school teachers when I changed class every year. I especially liked my teacher for the sixteen-year-olds and it was when I attended that class that I was finally baptized. Oh my, I learned so much from that teacher. It was not just the Bible that I learned, but she taught me so many other things that I needed to learn about at that time. Most of all, she never made me feel "less than" even though I came from a government home.

She helped to build my self-esteem in a lot of ways and in some ways helped me to start to understand about God's love, hope in God and how to start loving myself despite my situation, and what hope in God was really about. I still struggled with hopelessness and self-esteem because of the abuse I had gone through from the hand of my mother and the lack of love. All the pain I was carrying in my heart was so much, as I had not yet understood my life's journey, so I did experience constant struggles in rejection and lack of trust in anyone.

By now, I had some persons at this church who I could talk to about some of my struggles. One day, I decided to talk with one of the ladies from the mentorship group as I felt I could trust her. She invited me to her house, and for the first time, I shared some of my stories with her, detailing the abuse from my mother. It was so freeing just to be able to pour out my heart in that way. While sharing with that lady, I cried so hard; my eyes were swollen for days.

This experience was special as this was the first time I opened up so freely and was able to share with someone my hidden pain from the mountain of abuse I had gone through. The lady listened, and her response of encouragement was how important it would be for me to receive the baptism of the Holy Spirit, which is God's empowerment, providing me with His Helper so I could live more victoriously in my walk with Him.

Chapter 3
I Had No Father But God

One of the things that was a constant struggle and painful to me was the fact that I had no father to relate to. This hurt me deeply, and it still does, but learning about God and His promises helped me to understand that God is not only my Saviour and Lord, but He is my Father. However, this information or knowledge was not always easy for me to readily understand or relate to. The struggle was real, and I had to learn some hard lessons before I understood that God is the Father I never had.

Learning to relate to God as Father to this day is very challenging and not so easy at all; however, the experience has been rewarding. Just knowing that my heavenly Father understands me and I can talk to Him at any time about anything has really improved a lot, but the journey was not easy. This is especially true as I have no earthly father to help in the process, but God was there and is still with me daily. He came through for me in some awesome ways. One such example I remember was this one incident some years ago, when I needed some serious advice and was very worried about what I was going to do in making the decision. God led me to start figuring out what to do by just talking to Him about the situation. One Scripture I can remember that helped me is ***Jeremiah 33:3 - "Call to me and I will answer you and tell you great and unsearchable things you do not know."***

I would pray and pray and kept on praying. I did not always get the answer in the way I would like it, but God would certainly give me direction from His Word or send someone to discuss the situation and the decision that would need to be made. This was the first time I understood what it meant to pray and watch God work. One Scripture that helped me and gave me comfort was ***Psalm 20:1 - "May the Lord answer you when you are in distress; may the name of the God of Jacob protect you."***

Life is not easy at all, but without a father, a girl's life is rough. I struggled with feelings of not belonging, disconnection, and rejection. Life just did not feel real—not having that connection to a father or mother was hard. Whenever persons around me would talk about their family, especially their relationship with their father, I was jealous and secretly wished for what they had. My question to God was, "Why me?" This yearning for a father was made worse since my relationship with my mother was nil, even though I knew her.

As my relationship with God was developing, I realized from reading God's Word that God did love me, and He had a plan for my life. God did not randomly decide to love me; He chose me out of a deep passionate love. ***Deuteronomy 7:6 says - "The Lord your God has chosen you out of all the peoples on the face of the earth to be His people, His treasured possession."*** And in the Psalms, which brought me lots of comfort, one that I read a lot to this day is Psalm 139, especially **verse 2 - *"You know me when I sit and when I rise, you perceive my thoughts from afar."***

So even though I had feelings of isolation, rejection, and even feeling marginalized, with the stigma of growing in a government home and forgotten, I was now learning that I could live confidently knowing that

I am God's beloved child. I have a purpose, and God loves me. Now when I look at the enormity of the universe, even though I feel lost at times and still wonder about my purpose, I was slowly getting the understanding that there is purpose for my life.

Over the years, I have had many situations that would warrant my needing a father's or mother's support in my life, but God has stood by me as the Father I never had. I used to dread going to Fathers' Day service at church because of how sad that would make me feel, but over the years, I have come to celebrate my heavenly Father God whenever that service comes around. So, even though I never knew my earthly father, God has somehow helped me to understand Him as my heavenly Father. I can pray to Him and bring to Him all my expectations. He remains faithful, helping me in situations, especially when my need for a father arises. His Word has also given me much consolation. One verse of Scripture that has helped me to cope with this is ***Psalm 68:5 - "A Father to the fatherless, a defender of widows, is God in His holy dwelling."***

I cannot say I understand this Scripture totally, but I loved the fact that it spoke to me, in that God was the Father to the fatherless. This gave me some amount of hope and joy that it would be okay somehow, and I am going to be alright.

Chapter 4
Knowing God's Love

What is this love God wanted me to know from Him? I just did not comprehend it at all. Time and time again, I would ask God about His love for me. Since I could not understand God's love for me, I asked Him to help me understand His love. That was when He brought Ms. Fern into my life. She was one of the persons who came to visit and share with us children at the home. She would do lots of practical things for me, outside of praying and giving encouragement. My time at the home was made even better just knowing Ms. Fern. Looking back now, this was a measure of God's love I did not even comprehend at that time.

Life in the government home was ending. We had to leave at eighteen years old, and those of us who had family would be placed with them. Everything was rounding up my school years at Norman Manley High School. When school ended, I did not go to my graduation.

My mother had stayed in touch. She would visit me at the government home, sometimes. She, however, did not visit me very often, and when she did come, I did not speak with her much as I was very afraid of her. We never really bonded at all. I still remembered the abuse from her, so I did not want to go back to live with her.

Nearing my time to leave the home, Ms. Fern offered to help me. She found a place for me to live. This place was a boarding home in Stony Hill. She made all the arrangements and paid the boarding fee for a while. I still attended the church that Ms. Fern attended and formed a relationship with different persons there. I was close to one of my Sunday School teachers, and she found me a job at her sister's fabric store.

This, for me, was great and gave me a sense of independence. I thank the Lord now when I remember Ms. Fern for showing me God's love in such a powerful and practical way. She truly showed me the love of God. However, I struggled with lots of issues, and I did not know how to fit into society at that time. I now realize that I was living on the outside of myself, to appear normal and kept most things to myself. I still did not trust anyone easily, so even though I was in the church and should be happy and free, I was not. I felt I was still carrying a burden of some kind. I was misunderstood a lot, and my self-esteem was just nil, and I felt unfulfilled.

It was then that I started to visit other churches and started getting some other teaching in God's Word. One such teaching was about the Holy Spirit, who is our Helper in our walk with the Lord, and I said, "Wow! This is new information." I wanted to meet the Holy Spirit. I did not know or really understood then that I met Him the night I invited Jesus into my heart. I prayed to the Lord, asking Him to help me understand His Holy Spirit. As I visited this other church, I learned about the Holy Spirit and so many more gifts in the body of Christ.

One Sunday, when I attended that church, the speaker's message was on the Holy Spirit, using the Scripture in *Acts 1:8 - "But you will receive power when the Holy Spirit comes on you, and you will be my witnesses in Jerusalem, and in Judea and in Samaria, and to the ends of the earth."* After his sermon, he invited persons to the altar who wanted salvation and the baptism of the Holy Spirit. I went up for that prayer and prayed with that minister. However, I did not speak in tongues that day, but one day I did. You see, just as the minister had said, I eventually spoke in tongues as I had gotten the gift of the Holy Spirit, even as I had believed God by faith.

I continued reading the Word of God daily. The Word of God is so very encouraging to me. One Scripture that I kept meditating on was ***Acts 1:8a "But you will receive power when the Holy Spirit comes on you."***

One morning, in my devotional time with the Lord, I felt that extra something that I was yearning for was still missing. So I cried out to the Lord for more of Him, and the Lord did show up! It was then that I received the evidence of the baptism of the Holy Spirit. What a river it was! This experience was awesome, and the worship flowed. To this day, that time has remained so very special to me and, over the years, I keep on asking the Lord to fill me over and over again so I can live in His presence daily. I definitely need the Holy Spirit's help, and I have also learned that this gift comes in measures.

Chapter 5
Making A Difference

I always wanted to make a difference, and one of the things I felt from the Lord was the desire to pray for change in my church. This led to a prayer group being born in my church. This group consisted of seven ladies. We met weekly to share and pray. This was especially a very special time. We came from different walks of life, yet we had the same burden: we each wanted to see a change in our church.

God led us in some very special ways, and, over time, the group grew to about ten persons, and we saw God beginning to do some mighty things in our church. We saw the power of God revealed, and God showed up, answering our prayers in personal ways and in our church in some very specific ways. We experienced the hand of God, and our church grew. It was awesome. To this day, I believe some of those ladies continue to benefit from the answered prayers where God showed up in their lives, coming out of those prayer times we used to have.

It is important to note also that a group of men also met for prayer weekly. The ladies did not meet with the men. Both groups had started from different desires and promptings, and I think we were at different levels in our walk with the Lord, hence the separation. However, I believe God heard us all and answered all our prayers in many ways; the church took on many new activities, and God mightily showed up. We experienced much growth and new experiences in our church in those days.

I had moved from Stony Hill and was now living in Acadia in a rented one bedroom. I met a young lady there, and we became good friends. We shared with each other a lot, especially about the things of the Lord and our life's journey. By sharing and talking with her, I realized she had a lot of similar experiences like me, even though she grew up with her mother. The house I was living in was her big sister's foster mother's place, so she came on weekends to visit with her sister. This was the first person I can remember I really bonded with. She was a Christian, so we had much in common, and for that reason, we could share about our salvation and our desire to grow in God.

My friend, who we will call Nancy, talked with me about her high school boyfriend who went away to Canada and had not kept in touch with her. In talking with her, I realized she was deeply in love with that guy but did not want to own that as she was feeling hurt. As we talked, I encouraged her to write or call him and forgive him and let him know how she felt since he had started calling her, showing interest in her, even though he was living abroad. She eventually listened to my advice, and their friendship was rekindled in a significant way. They began to correspond often and developed their friendship and love for each other. They got married after a while and are still married to this day. This was one of the first amazing things to happen when I offered encouragement and prayer to someone who was hurting.

Another thing I became a part of, in the initial stage at my church, was making myself available to greet persons coming to church on Sundays. There was no usher ministry at that time. We only had a small building. The church was intimate at that time, and it felt like we all knew each other so very well.

I also taught a Sunday school class at my church, and this was another rewarding experience that was truly special for me. It gave me a sense of joy and true fulfillment. I taught the pre-teens, and it was quite interesting teaching that group of children. I found the experience to be interesting because of all the preparation to be made weekly. The children gave me such a push and a challenge as they often asked questions that needed answers. Every Sunday, the children came with many questions that we needed to have the correct answers for. This definitely pushed me to prepare to teach my Sunday school class of seven-year-olds.

There were two of us who taught that class at the time. The other teacher gave me the opportunity to teach often, even though we both enjoyed teaching the children. We both learned a lot from each other and from the children; we had so much fun and joy.

Chapter 6
Ordinary Made Extraordinary

There is so much I want to share with you. In this chapter, I want to tell of my experience in acquiring a great job, one that blew my mind. I was unemployed for about six months and kept sending out my resume, and all the responses I received basically said, "Sorry, no vacancy at this time."

Then one day, a lady I knew from church came to my house in Acadia and asked me for my resume. She told me God had sent her to find me and give me a job at a new bank that was opening in a month's time. I was in shock and could not believe this was actually happening for me.

I immediately went and got a copy of my resume and gave it to her. This lady, I will call her Miss Carlene, told me about the position and what it was all about. She explained to me right there what the job would involve, and the position I was being offered, and what would be expected of me.

Now, my only work experience up to that point in my life was working as a store clerk, where fabric and trimmings were sold. I did not have a whole lot of experience working in an office at all. In light of this new job offer, I really got excited and elated, and on my first day on the job, I felt then that I wanted to express my appreciation to the Lord in a special way and was inspired to write a poem to the Lord, which I will share with you.

> *Today God opened up for me an awesome miracle,*
> *From store clerk job to bank job;*
> *LORD, how great, awesome, and marvelous You are!*
> *You did this for me,*
> *I will never be able to comprehend this move of Yours towards me.*
>
> *Great, Great, Great God,*
> *You are good and You, God, are wonderful!*
> *Thanks, thanks, thanks to You, God.*

This first day at my new job at the bank,
Eagle Commercial Bank Limited,
I am in awe!
God, how blessed I feel
If this is how it feels, it is truly a wonderful and
an amazing feeling.

I feel to shout and sing at the same time,
To know You, Oh mighty God, have done this!
For me,
Thanks, thanks, thanks, to God ALMIGHTY!

What a mighty God You are,
You, God, still work miracles,
This job is one BIG Miracle and I thank You,
Lord
A bank job for me, wow!
Whoosh! Whew! I just bless Your Holy Name,
God!

My heart, my whole being is just so overjoyed,
And I feel happy, elated, to know You did this,
such a miracle for me to bring me to this great
job,

> *thanks, thanks, thanks to You, oh great*
> *sovereign Lord*
>
> *Truly, You are still in the business of seeing*
> *little people like me*
> *And allowing a big miracle like this,*
> *A job in a brand new bank.*
> *Thanks, thanks, thanks, mighty God.*
>
> *Bless the Lord, great King in Zion.*
> *Glory to the Most High God.*
> *Thanks, thanks, thanks to You, God.*

I was so grateful for my new job at the bank that I sang all the time; even my supervisor asked me why I was so happy all the time. She did not understand the reason why I was joyful. I had worked as a store clerk for seven years. Although I was happy, and could manage to pay my bills, I did not like that store job much. It did not provide me with a lot of challenges at all, and I cannot say I learnt anything much. In retrospect, that job at the store was a means to an end.

Eventually, I decided I could not stay; it was time to move on, so I resigned. I had worked there for seven years, not knowing where the next job would be; I took a step of faith. Thinking back now, maybe I should have sought to have discussions with a mentor but being the loner I was then, I did not think about that.

After I left that store clerk job, I was so sure I would have found a new job quickly, but that never happened. I learnt after that experience that it is better to start looking for a new job before leaving the old one.

I learnt many more lessons during that time of unemployment, which to this day has helped me in my walk with the Lord. I had to trust God to help me find my rent every month. Of course, my small savings helped, but I also learnt that God could take care of me in very practical ways.

My church was a good support through my Sunday School teacher, Ms. Nez. Ms. Nez played a special part in my growth spiritually, and she also made sure I was taken care of practically as well. I would go to church on Sundays to be surprised by her many times with gifts. She would have an envelope for me with cash and food items.

I was sometimes shocked and alarmed at this way of provision. It was surprising since I never asked her for anything. She just knew; hence, my food cupboard was regularly replenished, and some of the ladies in the prayer group I attended also gave support in practical ways with personal items. What a wonderful, amazing God we serve. I can emphatically say I really proved God's Word in **Philippians 4:19 - *"And my God will meet all my needs according to the riches of His glory in Christ Jesus."***

So, all these happenings gave me the inspiration to write that poem when I started my new job at the bank. It was just so wonderful to have come out of such experiences of working in a store, growing up in state care, and being unemployed for six months, and then landing a job in the bank, which God sent. None of those job applications I sent out prior had brought me a job; my heart was very grateful for what God had done for me.

The years I spent working at the bank were great, with lots of exciting and happy moments, for the most part. It had many challenges, also many teaching and growth experiences and, most of all, I gained lots of confidence about my self-worth and self-confidence.

Before I knew it, the years had flown by, and a decade had gone. There were lots of uncertainty going on in the banking sector then that caused me to think about resigning. Then the thought of my purpose, which had always been on my mind, for a while, began to burn even brighter, begging for attention.

God showed up and started speaking to my heart about my true purpose, and I honestly thought He was leading me to another move for change towards His purpose.

God can restore life's purpose and give hope to those who are broken; a part of me wanted to do that more than anything else.

Chapter 7
God's Purpose For My Life

One of my favorite hobbies in those days was reading. One of the books I found myself enjoying was "The Purpose Driven Life" by Rick Warren. I could identify with a lot of what I read, and the very first chapter was dealing with one question I asked myself often, "Why am I here?" So along with reading that book and my Bible, which I so love reading, I realized that God had a purpose for my life, and I wanted to know what that purpose was.

I began to pray about that and asked the Lord to reveal what my purpose was. After seeking the Lord on this issue, I began to feel this need to help hurting people. I was always drawn to persons who hurt, especially those persons hurting emotionally. I could sit and listen to someone share about issues that cause them to hurt for hours on end and would not feel tired to listen.

It did not become clear how I was to do this. However, I kept praying and seeking the Lord. By that time, I had been working in the bank for about ten years and felt the need for more. I did not get true clarity until I attended one of the yearly Missions Conferences at my church. The speaker spoke about **"Launching Out Into The Deep."** The message was very direct for me, and I felt God was asking me to take a step of faith in trying to touch those who are hurting, and, to this day, I sense my calling is to people who have been hurt deeply and still carry some form of hurt.

I went to the altar that night, which was the final night of the Conference. I shared what I felt in my heart with the counselor and what God was saying to me, and how the message that night had touched me. I was then prayed for. At that time, the banking sector was going through some unstable times, and persons in my organization were being made redundant. You were either chosen or you could request your redundancy. So that was what I did: I requested my redundancy, thinking this was my step of faith to launch into the deep. I still had no idea what was yet to come.

About two months later, after I had received my redundancy from the bank, I still had no idea where I would find people to help, especially since I felt my call was for hurting people. One day I received a call from the then president of the Jamaica Youth for Christ (JYFC). He invited me to come help out at his office in a voluntary position. As I recall, he said to me there was much work to do, but not a lot of money for a salary, and he was gearing up to start a new program for students, so I figured I could start there. I knew nothing about the JYFC ministry, but I was so eager and happy for this opportunity I was getting, so I did some research to get information on them and what they were about, and what their offerings were.

On the day I went for the interview, I met with the president and heard more of what JYFC does and what they were all about. I also learned that there would be no proper salary like I was used to. They would, however, cover my bus fare and give a small stipend, which would be given to me weekly as they were not in a position to offer any pay. "Wow!" I said to myself, "This was going to be very interesting" and a challenge, but my desire to serve was real, and that was all I wanted to do. I was prepared to trust God for my support, so I decided that I would go ahead there for three days each week, doing what they wanted me to do and trust God. One Scripture that I took very literally, as I started on this path, was **Proverbs 3:5-6 "Trust in the Lord with all your heart and lean not on your own understanding. In all your ways submit to Him, and He will make your paths straight."**

One of the plans they had then was to start and run a Counselling Centre. When I joined the JYFC team, this was not happening yet. This, I thought, was my opening to do something extraordinary for God. One Scripture that I was reminded of then was *Philippians 4:13 - "I can do all things through Christ who gives me strength."* With that in mind, I was able to write the programme for after-school students to include counseling for those children with their parent(s). I cannot remember if we had to do much advertisement, but we had the children from the immediate community coming to the Counseling Centre to be a part of the programme. There began the JYFC Counseling Centre situated in the Cross Roads area.

The programme was set up with a partnership put in place to have students who were studying counseling psychology do their practicum at Jamaica Youth for Christ, counseling the children and their parents at

JYFC Counseling Centre. The children not only came from the immediate community, but we got referrals from schools as far as the Papine area. The programme grew rapidly, and it brought me so much joy to serve those children who hurt in so many ways.

That was certainly one thing I have done in my life to this day that I have enjoyed very much. I did not earn a salary, but God provided. That time was one of the best times in my life and one of the hardest. Let us face it, I had bills to pay and monthly expenses to deal with. By now, God had raised up a few supporters for me, my church being one of them. God did some really awesome things.

The Counseling Centre had about fifty children: boys and girls. We, however, had more boys. We hosted parenting seminars. We took the children on field trips. God gave direction as to how they were to be taught about God and how to pray, and we had a theme: **"Respect and Love."**

The children came mostly from the inner city from the Cross Roads area. They were each assigned a counselor to help them work through their issues. They had lots of behavioural issues, and it was truly challenging, but I enjoyed this challenge very much, seeing and working with the children. As they came into their own and changed, especially where their social skills were concerned, it was great.

The Counseling Centre operated under the umbrella of the Jamaica Youth for Christ. It operated three days per week and started mid-morning to facilitate the children when they left school. This was mostly to facilitate mentorship in every area of their lives. We began each day with devotions with the children, and it would always be surrounded by our theme: "**Respect and Love.**" The children were often encouraged to lead in the devotional exercise. This would help to build their confidence. This was the routine of the Counseling Centre, which ran for about eight and a half years. Then God began to show me, in many different ways, that the assignment was coming to an end. Firstly, we had someone who paid our security officer's fees weekly withdraw that support. Another donor could not be found. The operations of the Centre ended at about 9 PM most nights, and the area was lonely so having security in the night was critical. Secondly, the counselors were leaving as most of them had finished their studies and no new ones were coming in to give their time. Those who had graduated were not able to continue to support the programme. A few counselors had finished prior and were still supporting the programme, but many were not able to continue much longer. Those were some of the signs that told me the assignment was coming to an end.

After much prayer and consideration, I resigned from my job at the JYFC in 2010. Sad to say, when I left Jamaica Youth for Christ, the program did not continue much longer. However, to this day, I do believe that the assignment at Jamaica Youth for Christ in that counseling Centre helped hurting people. We had lots of adults come in for counseling as well. It was one of my best times working with those children.

I made contact with some of the parents of those children; most of them are young adults now, and I was happy to learn how well most of them were doing.

Conclusion

In closing, I can say I have overcome in many ways. God has healed many things in my life and heart that have brought me to a place to feel restored. Working with those children in the mentorship program at JYFC gave me lots of peace, joy, and healing, so after I left, I continued seeking the Lord for my next assignment/job, which led me to work in the church.

God taught me that even though I did not know my earthly father, He, God, was the Father I can depend on. My emotional healing started and continues; it is a process, and I have more confidence in God that He will guide and help me in all I do. The road I take daily is leaning on the Lord, trusting, and most of all, believing what He said in His Word that He will do, and I choose to stand on His promises daily. Please know anything is possible with God being on your side, so trust Him.

I will leave with you some scripture verses that have helped me:

***Isaiah 43:19 (NIV)** "See, I am doing a new thing! Now it springs up; do you not perceive it? I am making a way in the wilderness and streams in the wasteland."*

***Psalm 20:4 (NIV)** "May he give you the desire of your heart and make all your plans succeed."*

Be blessed!

About the Author

Pauline M. Dillon is a driven and detail-oriented professional with over twenty years of experience in Administration; she is adept at managing and streamlining with the ability to complete any task assigned. Her vision is to provide care counseling to revitalize and energize hurting situations through Jesus Christ, encouraging hope to persons from all walks of life, especially those who are hurting, wounded in spirit, in despair, and hopeless (See Isaiah 58:12).

www.ingramcontent.com/pod-product-compliance
Lightning Source LLC
Chambersburg PA
CBHW070107100426
42743CB00012B/2676